BETTER
HUMAN
IT'S A FULL-TIME JOB.

 BY RONDA CONGER

Mom, I love you.

CONTENTS

PREFACE

I recently read an article that talked about the people who write books and speak in public about *being better* – self improvement if you will. They do it first and foremost for themselves.

I believe it.

This book is a reminder that I am far from done. That I am a full-time job.

I'm like you. I want better. I want more. I want to get it all. I work hard to be a better human, wife, mother, entrepreneur, friend and hustler.

My wish for you and this book is that it moves you to be better in whatever arena you choose. I coined this book *Better Human* because it all starts with YOU.

Better human starts today.

– Ronda Conger

Never stop believing that."

— Daddy Warbucks

IT'S A HARD KNOCK LIFE

CHAPTER ONE
IT'S A **HARD KNOCK LIFE**

There are so many different ways I could introduce myself to you. So let's make it the most fun we can and do it Broadway musical style. I want you to sing along with me as I give you a quick and dirty little run down of why I am on a never-ending pursuit to be a **BETTER HUMAN**. I realized a long, long, long, long (okay, I am not that old) time ago that becoming a better human is, well, a full-time job. To be better, you have to fight, focus, commit believe and, most importantly, never give up on the notion that you can be better. You can.

I have to believe that you are like me. That you have picked up this book for a reason. That you, too, are on the hunt.

Welcome to the journey, my friend, welcome.

The first song that sums up my early years would be from the Broadway musical Annie: Perhaps you know the words to *It's a Hard Knock Life?* Please pay close attention to correct pitch, arm movements, appropriate posture and the necessary swagger when belting out: "IT'S A HARD KNOCK LIFE."

Try it.

IT'S A HARD KNOCK LIFE...
IT'S A HARD KNOCK LIFE!!

Back at that age, I connected with Annie. She got me. Her life in the beginning was the pits. But I thought, if she could sing through it all, why couldn't I? After all, the sun will come out tomorrow? Right? Tomorrow, I love ya...(Tell me you are singing with me).

Let's start with the basics and cue up a brief highlight reel on my life so you can understand this thirst, this passion for better. My mother died in a car crash when I was 3 years old. Don't break out the tissues quite yet. She's with me every minute. I talk to her every day. I choose to focus on what she gave me (life), on three years together, on my blue eyes, on knowing that I am making her proud. I like to think that my life from age zero to three was some of the best of times. My husband would tell you my mom made me the warrior I am today.

After the age of three, it was a downhill slide but remember the SUN WILL COME OUT TOMORROW or, in my case, at the beautiful age of 17. I realized early on that I had a knack for knowing what I wanted to have in my life – and what I did not. I don't want to bore you with the drama of it all, so let's just say that the parade of people in my life during that time span was colorful. Usually, when I speak in front of large groups, I try to explain that, by all rights, I should be the poster child for the kid who ends up in a roadside ditch.

The theatrics that come with numerous step-mothers, divorces, step-siblings, drugs in and around me, the physical and mental abuse and innumerable other follies made for one hell of a childhood. I was twice kicked to the curb with the last time during my senior year of high school. My nanny (a.k.a. Grandmother), took me in for a short time. I pushed myself and I mean PUSHED myself to get through that year of high school to graduate. I received my diploma with not one person in the stands. No one weeping tears of joy, no one frantically snapping photos, no rows of family smiling and waving.

I WAS THE SOLE PERSON IN THE RONDA FAN CLUB THAT DAY AND I REALIZED THEN THAT IT WAS ALL ON ME. **BEST DAMN NEWS I HAD EVER HEARD.**

My father is an amazing man. My love for him is like no other. I love all that is good and all that is bad and really bad. You don't get to choose; you just have to take it all. It took me ten years to figure that out. Ten years to learn that anger and resentment will never heal you, never push you forward, never let you go. Even though he was messy, he did try to fill me up with words of wisdom even when his actions did not match. Some of my favorites were: "Pretty is as pretty does," "Hang with a dog and you are a dog," "If you're not the lead dog, the view never changes," and "Go for the gold."

"KNOCK OFF YOUR REAR VIEW MIRRORS

But my favorite would have to be: "Knock off your rear view mirrors and never look back." He always has been a hard working, hard charging, passionate man and I thank him for sharing those traits with me. As for the rest of his traits and behaviors, I will pass.

Don't get me wrong. I am thankful for all of it. The good, the bad, the ugly, and the evil. I learned to focus on making sure that I would be none of those things I left behind and I knew that I would be better. I could do it.

The sun did come out and I have had some amazing people in my life who were my rocks that pushed me, that never let me feel sorry for myself, never let me settle, never let me get sucked into the muck of it all.

At the beautiful age of 17, I knocked off my rear view mirrors and drove it like I stole it. With a backpack and a passport I boarded a plane to Canada where I held up to four jobs at one time. Every minute was spoken for. I had food to buy, rent to pay, and gas to put in the tank. I snuck in school when I could. There were community college courses and books, sweet glorious books.

Reading was always an escape for me when I was younger. It helped me get away from my less-than-stellar life. I was a voracious reader. I could not get enough. That passion revealed to me that books would show me a better life. A better me.

I attended community college and university as I hunted for this life, this better human. I worked as hard as I possibly could.

As I look back now I realize that are a few strong principles that have guided my life. I call them *Ronda-isms* and I share them with everyone I come in contact with. I want to help, share my love, my struggle, my knowledge.

The beauty of life is that you get to start each day anew. Each day, you get to awaken to the opportunity to find your better human. It's something I fight for and work for every day.

I am a full-time job.

I am far from done.

The kid who was supposed to be in the ditch has two amazing sons, a husband of 25 years, is the Vice President of the largest homebuilder in Idaho, owner of a real estate firm and now the author of this book.

I WANT THIS BOOK TO BE A GIFT FROM ME TO YOU AND TO BE AN ADVENTURE. *a wild ride.* A FLAT GOOD TIME.

We are going to laugh, cry, Google, listen to playlists, read blogs and check out books that I love. Buckle up. Arms and hands in the ride at all times. It's going to be a wild one.

Better human starts today.

"**Love** is choosing to accept someone — imperfections, weaknesses, demands and all — no matter his or her circumstances or needs."

— Mark Sanborn

CHAPTER TWO
THERE IS ONLY **LOVE**

When you operate from love, everything changes. The way you see your life, the people in it, where you work. *Everything.* Hate begets hate. Love begets love.

I've always said that the only thing I want in life is love. I put as much love as I can out there. I love my car, I love my shoes, I love my house, I love my children, I love my husband, I love the people I work with each and every day.

Think of someone you love right now. Think about how you treat them. How you feel about them. How you get excited when you see them. You would move mountains for them. You smile the minute they walk in the door. You hug them and, if you're anything like me, you tell them you love them often. You're excited to be in their presence. You just feel better because of them.

Simple question for you:

DON'T YOU WANT THAT KIND OF FEELING AND LOVE

IN EVERY INSTANCE?

Hence the chapter title, there is only love. In all instances. Give me one reason you wouldn't want to have those kinds of feelings and actions in your daily life.

I firmly believe that most people walk around with three percent of love and 97 percent of the "not so fast" attitude toward people and life. I would love to change that as did Ghandi and, of course, Mother Teresa.

Don't get me wrong; I am no saint. But at the wise age of 17, I realized that I get to choose who is in my life. Choose wisely, my friend; choose the people who fill up your tank. People who deserve your love.

LOVE TAKES WORK.
TAKES TIME.
NEEDS ATTENTION.
EVERY DAY.

Love, when you get it right, should be found at home, at work, with your friends, and in your day-to-day life. It starts with you. What are you putting out there?

We are dealing with a boomerang. Whatever you throw out to the world is coming right back to you. WHAM. Are you excited for it? Or cringing?

I have two exercises for you. Let's test this whole boomerang theory.

Next time you are at the check out stand and the cashier does not smile, say hello, or acknowledge your existence, do me a favor. Stop, smile, ask them how they are and find one thing about them that is awesome. Then, tell them. The response will be magical. They will light up, thank you and possibly even hug you. We can always hope.

If you have teenagers in and around you and they are less than welcoming, loving or chipper in your presence, stop and hug them. Instead of ignoring them, rolling your eyes, or giving them the excuse that they are a teenager and all act this way. Do the whole back hug thing if you have to. Then keep doing it until they realize you love them and you are not going to stop based on their actions. Mess with the boomerang theory until you get what you want back.

LOVE IS NOT EASY OR PERFECT, BUT IT IS **POWERFUL BEYOND ALL MEASURE.**

Two of my favorite football coaches have had their ups and downs. Good news, they're human. I still love them. Remember, people are messy.

I just watched Ohio State beat Oregon in the College Football National Championship game. It was a beautiful thing. I am a HUGE Urban Meyer fan. They interviewed Meyer, who is the head coach for Ohio State, right after the game. While the streamers were still flying, the fans were rushing the field, the players were hugging and celebrating. The reporter grabbed the Coach in the middle of the field and asked, "What does it feel like to win a national championship?" Meyer answered, "I want to share it with the guys. I love these guys."

 www.betterhuman.today/pages/**urbanmeyerESPN**

Urban Meyer is a man under construction. For the last three years he has been trying to find the meaning of life, to find love, to spend time with his family, and to appreciate his players. He has a long way to go. You can be a critic but I like what I'm seeing. Loving what you do and who you do it with looks good on him.

My other favorite example of love on the football field is Pete Carroll, the head coach of the Seattle Seahawks. I read an article called, "Given a Choice, Players Pick Carroll." They polled all of the players in the NFL and asked, if given the choice, which head coach would you most like to play for? They picked Pete Carroll. Here's why:

"That's largely because Carroll has mastered the art of giving everything of himself and baring his soul as much as any head coach can. It's a rare feat for any man running an NFL team to attempt..."

A few years back I found an awesome clip called the voices of the NFL coaches. It showed a highlight reel of several NFL coaches on the sidelines. Some of the coaches were kicking water bottles, screaming, cussing, and throwing their clipboards. And then there was Pete Carroll.

He was high fiving, hugging, and kissing their foreheads; you could see him telling one of his guys, "I love you, man."

Yes, he has a past, yes it was messy. Get in line. He has cleaned house, taken his team to two Super Bowls with the entire NFL wanting him as a coach. He figured it out.

All he needed was love. Love for his life, his career, and his team.

Magic, I tell you, magic.

My goal is to give you random examples of love and winning with love in some of the most unexpected places. There are no excuses why you would not change your programming. Why you would not operate with love from this day forward. Love wins.

How about Joel Manby? He is the President and CEO of Herschend Family Entertainment Corporation, which is the largest family-owned theme park corporation in the U.S. He became famous in 2010 when he was featured on the CBS hit show *Undercover Boss*. He then wrote one of my all-time favorite books called *Love Works*. **Yes, it does.** His whole leadership and life philosophy and success have been because of love.

READ THIS *Love Works* by Joel Manby

I leave you with this teaser from the book:

"Treating someone with love regardless of how you feel about that person is a very powerful principle . . . It can make us great spouses, great parents, and great friends. Great leaders, too."

YOUR WORDS ARE POWERFUL.
Keep them full of love.

I tell everyone I love them. I do. I am that girl. I was shopping last week at Lululemon hoping to replace my favorite pair of yoga pants. I had the pleasure of meeting a young gal who offered to help me. She said she knew exactly what I was looking for. I told her she was spectacular. She then had a small problem with finding the correct size, did a quick search in the back and BAM she reappeared with my favorite leggings. I, in turn, professed my love for her.

I literally said I love you! Do you want to know what she said back to me?

First, she hugged me and then said I made her day.

Whose day have you made lately?

How many times have you said **I love you**?

xoxo

Let's talk about your health and love.

I found an article online by a Dr. Kim. He wrote an insightful article called, "How important is love to your health?"

"In addressing lifestyle factors that influence health, it is important to consider food choices, exercise, rest, and environmental factors like fresh air and sunlight. Scientists are beginning to discover that there is one facet of life that ranks above all of these factors in determining wellness and longevity. This facet is the level of love and connectedness that we feel."

DID YOU READ THAT?!?!?!
LOVE ranks above all of these factors.

> Google this ▸ Why is love important?

When I speak in front of large groups, I make them "hug it out" before I begin my presentation.

Here is an excerpt from one of my favorite theories on love and the benefits of hugging:

TEN REASONS WHY WE NEED EIGHT HUGS A DAY
By Marcus Julian Felicetti

Research shows a proper deep hug, where the hearts are pressing together, can benefit you in these ways:

1. The nurturing touch of a hug builds trust and a sense of safety. This helps with open and honest communication.

2. Hugs can instantly boost oxytocin levels, which heal feelings of loneliness, isolation and anger.

3. Holding a hug for an extended time lifts one's serotonin levels, elevating mood and creating happiness.

4. Hugs strengthen the immune system.

5. Hugging boosts self-esteem. From the time we're born our family's touch shows us that we're loved and special. Hugs, therefore, connect us to our ability to self-love.

6. Hugging relaxes muscles. Hugs release tension in the body. Hugs can take away pain; they soothe aches by increasing circulation into the soft tissues.

7. Hugs balance out the nervous system.

8. Hugs teach us how to give and receive. There is equal value in receiving and being receptive to warmth, as to giving and sharing. Hugs educate us how love flows both ways.

9. Hugs are so much like meditation and laughter. They teach us to let go and be present in the moment. They encourage us to flow with the energy of life.

10. The energy exchange between the people hugging is an investment in the relationship. It encourages empathy and understanding.

There is an article by Virginia Satir, a respected family therapist that says, "'We need **four** hugs a day for survival. We need **eight** hugs a day for maintenance. We need **twelve** hugs a day for growth." Eight or more might seem quite high, but while researching and writing this article I asked my child, "How many hugs a day do you like?" She said, "I'm not going to tell you how many I like, but its way more than eight.'"

I find that LOVE is a miracle drug.

Love is game changer.

Love takes something from average to something amazing. When you give love people notice it. They want more of it.

Love is what we all crave. It's why we are here. Love wins.

When you show and give your love to your family, to your work, to your friends, to strangers, it comes back to you two fold. Same goes for anger, hate and resentment.

I think about this in each interaction with all of those I come in contact with. What do I want from them?

I want love. How about you?

> ONE WORD FREES US OF ALL THE WEIGHT AND PAIN OF LIFE. **THE WORD IS LOVE.** — Sophocles

Add love into all areas of your life.

Sign your emails with "love" versus "sincerely." Say "I love you" when you say good-bye at the end of a call.

I recently started signing all my emails:
"Love You Madly, Ronda Conger."

Completely freaks some people out. But those who know me understand why I do it.

Give it a whirl. Make someone's day.

"You simply will not be the same person
TWO MONTHS FROM NOW
after consciously giving thanks each day for
the abundance that exists in your life.
And you will have set in motion an
ancient spiritual law:
THE MORE YOU HAVE AND ARE GRATEFUL FOR,
THE MORE WILL BE **GIVEN** YOU."

— Sarah Ban Breathnach

CHAPTER THREE
GRATEFUL HEART

You see we have it all wrong. We are in the habit of only saying thank you when it is in our favor. When something is good for you. When it goes your way. We have it all wrong.

Life is a gift. All of it.

Every second, every breath, every moment, everything we have is a gift. It means we are still here. It means we need to be thankful.

Have you said **thank you** today?

I heard this incredible story recently about Matthew Henry, the famous Bible scholar. He was once accosted by thieves and robbed of his money.

He wrote these words in his diary:

Let me be thankful . . .
First, because I was never robbed before.
Second, although they took my purse they didn't take my life.
Third, because, although they took my all, it wasn't much.
Fourth, because it was I who was robbed, not I who robbed.

A GRATEFUL HEART IS AN **AMAZING GIFT.**

A grateful heart is about having perspective in all things. It is easy to say thank you when all is in your favor. How about when it is not? How do you look at your life? When in doubt reread Henry's poem above.

Last Thanksgiving we attended our church service and the message was spot on. You have to know that I am "that person" who takes notes during church.

So glad I did.

Before I tell you the story, I must share a secret about myself. Something I know is a direct correlation with my success in life.

Are you **ready** for it?

I WRITE EVERYTHING DOWN.

YOU WILL NEVER FIND ME WITHOUT A PEN AND PAPER.

EVER.

Greatness is in and around you. Be ready to take note of it. To learn from it. To share it. If I did not write down what I heard that day I would not be able to share it with thousands of people. I have used it in no less than five presentations, handed it out to hundreds of people and now you are reading it in my book.

Getting back to the Thanksgiving message: Mark Russell, the former Missions Pastor at my church, shared with the audience *How Not To Be Thankful.*

Talk about a funny perspective.

We are always getting told to be thankful or how to be thankful but never have I heard it put in such a fashion.

Here's his list:

HOW TO NOT BE THANKFUL

sense of ENTITLEMENT. YOU DESERVE ONLY GOOD THINGS.

TOO BUSY *TO BE* thankful

YOU HAVE A PRECONCEIVED IDEA OF HOW LIFE IS SUPPOSED TO BE. UPSET WHEN IT DOESN'T LINE UP THE **WAY YOU WANT.**

INCREASED EASE DOES NOT CAUSE **THANKFULNESS.** you are less appreciative when you are comfy.

YOU DON'T TAKE THE TIME OR THE EYES TO SEE IT.

YOU FEEL LIFE IS DIFFICULT.

BITTERNESS OVER OUR PAST PREVENTS US FROM SEEING BEAUTY IN THE PRESENT.

① YOU DON'T THINK ABOUT THE ROLES PEOPLE PLAY IN OUR LIVES. YOU THINK YOU WERE **SELF-MADE.**

UR SELF-ABSORBED.

THINGS AREN'T ALWAYS **GOOD** and you think they should be.

– Mark Russell

DOWNLOAD THIS **FREEBIE** PLEASE SHARE BY ALL MEANS.

www.betterhuman.today/pages/**howtonotbethankful**

Do a personal audit on the items listed. How we doing? The only way I can survive my past is to be thankful for all of it. The hardships have taught me that I am a warrior. Not a victim. A warrior. A victim asks why me? It says I don't deserve this. The warrior says I can handle it. I can be better because of this. Warriors say thank you.

I have had some pretty evil people in my life who did whatever they could to tear me down. I am thankful for them. They taught me how not to behave. They taught me that I can survive. They taught me that life is all about perspective.

What you seek is what you find. What are you looking for? Find the good. Let the not so good go. Learn from both. Focus on this breath, this moment. You are alive. What more could you be but thankful? I am thankful for it all. The good, the bad, the evil. I can't be picky. I won't be a victim.

Reason 5,002 my husband thinks I walk on water is because I am a HUGE ESPN fan. I mean HUGE.

One of my favorite moments was NBA's Kevin Durant's MVP speech.

 www.betterhuman.today/pages/**kevindurantMVP**

What a beautiful speech. We could all learn from it. He took all seven minutes of his MVP speech to talk about EVERYONE but himself. He gets it. He personally thanked each of his teammates, his coaches, and his mother. It was not an acceptance speech, it was a thank you speech.

I filled out a personal questionnaire last week and it asked me to list something that no one knows about me. I wrote:

I pray and say thank you all day.

I do. It keeps me focused. It keeps me grounded. It keeps me humble.

There are all sorts of ways to have a grateful heart.

Here are a few of my favorites:

- Keep a gratitude journal
- Use a gratitude app
- Each day, post on your desk five things you are grateful for.
  Do it **every day** for 365 days.

- Put 10 blank notecards on your desk or by your phone each week. By the end of the week, send out thank you cards to 10 new people.
The response will overwhelm you.

Do this:

I need you to give this whole grateful heart thing a go.

Write down three things that you are grateful for,
right here, right now.

1.

2.

3.

Here are my three:

THANK YOU FOR **YOU**.
THANK YOU FOR ANOTHER DAY TO GET IT RIGHT.
THANK YOU FOR CHEETOS.

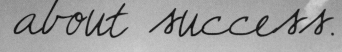

"*I never dreamed about success.*
I WORKED FOR IT."

— Estée Lauder

CHAPTER FOUR

NOTHING WORKS
UNTIL YOU DO

Get the F*@% out of bed. Sleep early. Do your work. Improve every day. Explore new things. And just get out of bed. This is an excerpt from one of my favorite prints that I have hanging in my office.

It's a proven fact that morning people are **HAPPIER** and are more satisfied overall with life.

GET THE F*@% OUT OF BED.

sleep f*@%ing early.
do your f*@%ing work.
get a damn workout.
improve everyday.
meet new f*@%ing people.
explore new things.

and just get the f*@% out of bed.

DOWNLOAD THIS **FREEBIE** PLEASE SHARE BY ALL MEANS.

www.betterhuman.today/pages/**getoutofbed**

I have Googled it several times and one of my favorites is an article that lists 29 successful people who wake up early.

The list included Richard Branson. Of course, it did. Before I forget, please read his book *Screw It, Let's Do It*. He gets it. "Screw it, let's do it," is now a crucial part of my vocabulary and can be found behind 99.9 percent of all my decisions.

My soon to be friend, Tony Robbins, is on the list. Duh.

Let's throw in Disney's CEO, Starbucks' CEO, Pepsi's CEO and the editor of *Vogue* for good measure.

Success leaves tracks. This is not rocket science. Get up.

I love when people tell me that their diet didn't work, their exercise program sucks, they didn't hit their sales goals, and their marriage is in the tanker. I call rubbish on the whole thing. Say it with me. **RUBBISH.**

We are all waiting for the magic pill. The lottery ticket of all lottery tickets. The secret of all secrets to whatever success we can dream of.

Drum roll please...

NOTHING WORKS UNTIL YOU DO.

Peyton Manning and Gatorade teamed up to make a commercial that says it best.

You don't sweat it. You don't get it.

 www.betterhuman.today/pages/**sweatittogetit**

I have had a job since I was 12 years old and have never looked back. I used to scoop ice out of ice machines and put them in plastic bags for twenty-five cents per bag. Talk about a grind. I averaged approximately five bags per hour. When I wasn't bagging ice, I would stand in the middle of Main Street with a jar of pepperoni samples and hand them to cars as they drove by.

I am a worker.

My college days found me working up to four jobs at one time. I had a lifestyle to maintain and a strong desire for more. The only way any of those things where going to happen was if I worked for it.

No one was handing me anything. No silver spoon, no free rides. I enjoyed the grind. I enjoyed the climb.

You have to be willing to sweat it. Every diet that I actually followed – worked. Every exercise program where I actually did the work, worked. Every job I've worked, I've excelled. Simple math.

I work on my marriage every day. It's a full-time job and a beautiful thing. It works and so do I. My hot-as-sin husband and I created this list called, **"LOVE IS HERE TO STAY."** It's a list of things that we work on each and every day.

 DOWNLOAD THIS FREEBIE PLEASE SHARE BY ALL MEANS.

www.betterhuman.today/pages/**loveisheretostay**

Love is here to STAY

Spend *more time* with your spouse than your friends.

Hold hands **always**. *Never stop.*

A man's success is in direct proportion to his wife's confidence in him.

Tell your wife she's *beautiful* every day.

Spend more time focusing on **why you love each other** than what needs to be fixed.

Court her. Send her flowers. Go on **dates**. Send love notes.

Court him. Get **hot** for him. Send love notes.

Say "I love you" at **every** opportunity.

Don't fight about money. *It's never worth it.* Never.

It's not about you. It's about **us**.

Laugh. **A lot.**

Your life is a full-time job. **Being a better human is a full-time job.** I have come to realize that we could eliminate a few key items in our day-to-day lives that are game changers and, at times, hinder our ability to do the work.

Here's a list of what doesn't work:

- Watching mind-numbing TV. It's time to break up with Snooki.
- Spending hours on social media. Tweet you later.
- Sleeping your life away. It's embarrassing.
- Indulging the bad vices that do not serve you or your body. Enough said.
- Continuing relationships with people who do not share the same level of goals and expectations. See ya', sailor.

YOU WANT **DIFFERENT**?
YOU WANT **MORE**?
YOU DREAM OF **BETTER**?

The definition of insanity is doing the same thing over and over again, and still expecting a different result.

Are you doing more? Better? Different?

Here's my more, better, different list:

- Read any and all that pushes you to be better.
- Watch only those things that uplift you.
- Learn from those who have been successful.
- Work Hard. Really hard. No clock punching.
- Give more than what is expected. Be that guy.
- Smile at everyone. It takes work.
- Love it all. Enjoy the ride.
- Be grateful that you get another day to work. Another day to get it right.

I crush all over Sam Parker of Givemore.com. That guy gets it. He wrote a book and started a movement called Smile and Move. Brilliant. Just brilliant. Visit www.smileandmove.com and buy the book. Every new employee at my day job is given a copy of *Smile and Move*, just in case there is any grey in what we expect them to do.

One of my most popular presentations is called:

ARE YOU A PILOT OR A PASSENGER?

Well, which is it?

Let's look at the definition of both before you decide:

pi·lot (pīʹlət)

a. The helmsman of a ship.

b. To serve as the pilot of a vessel.

c. To steer or control the course of.

pas·sen·ger (păsʹən-jər)

a. A person who travels in a conveyance, without participating in its operation.

b. A person who participates only passively in an activity.

Oh, boy! You know I am going to have a field day with this one. If you are not doing the work, if you are passively participating in your life or not at all, then you, my friend, are a passenger.

Stop now and get off the train.

This is your life. You are meant to be a pilot. You are meant to be at the helm of your ship, to steer, to control, to work.
You will not be passive.
You will work for it.
You will sweat for it.
Nothing works until you do.

"THE BIGGEST **HURDLE** IN LIFE IS GETTING OVER **YOURSELF.** ONCE YOU GET OVER YOURSELF, **YOU CAN GET ANYWHERE!"**

–TONY GASKINS

CHAPTER FIVE
GET OVER **YOURSELF**

Hold up, sailor. You may be thinking to yourself...this chapter is not for me.

Yes, yes it is. I will put money on it.

Take my GET OVER YOURSELF quiz below before you decide to skip this chapter.

If you answer *yes* to one of the questions, you, my friend, need to get over yourself.

GET OVER YOURSELF QUIZ

- DO YOU FEEL LIKE YOU HAVE "ARRIVED" IN LIFE?

- DO YOU FEEL LIKE YOU ARE AT THE TOP OF YOUR GAME?

- ARE YOU THE SMARTEST PERSON YOU KNOW?

- DO YOU DISLIKE CRITICISM?

- DO YOU BELIEVE YOU ARE PERFECT?

- DO YOU MAKE A LOT OF MONEY?

- DO YOU THINK YOUR LIFE IS MISERABLE? THAT IT'S NOT FAIR?

- DO YOU THINK YOU ARE THE ONLY ONE WITH PROBLEMS?

- ARE YOU CONSTANTLY THINKING ABOUT YOUR ROUGH CHILDHOOD?

- DO YOU HAVE BAD LUCK?

- ARE YOU A CONTROL FREAK?

- ARE YOU THE ONLY ONE WHO IS CAPABLE OF DOING ANYTHING RIGHT? EVER?

Getting over yourself comes in all sorts of packages. Were you surprised by the list above?

Self-absorption, an out-of-control ego, all about you and your world thinking, and your permanent lifetime pass on the pity train qualifies you for this chapter.

Each of us has a messy life to some degree. We all have room for more; room for growth and the need to reach out to others.

Try something for me: Ask the next three people you encounter about three things that are a struggle for them. Whether it is current, from the past, or from their childhood.

This just in:

WE ALL HAVE SOMETHING.

Now do this: Ask three people you know well and who will be honest with you, to name three things you could improve upon. If they have nothing to say, call them Pinocchio and go find an honest friend.

IN ORDER TO GET OVER
YOURSELF, YOU NEED TO
RECOGNIZE YOU ARE NOT THE
ONLY PERSON IN THE WORLD
*and you have room
for improvement*
(ALWAYS).

Did you know that Bill Gates, the owner and magician of Microsoft, goes away every year for two weeks to read by himself? He wants to be better. Be smarter. Have more.

How about this? Darren Hardy of *Success* magazine interviewed hundreds of CEOs from the Top 100 Fortune 500 Companies in the world.

He narrowed to three, the things they all have in common:

1 THEY ARE **RELENTLESS** IN THEIR LEARNING

2 THEY READ **FIVE** BOOKS A MONTH

3 THEY SET **GOALS**

WE CAN ALL BE *better.* WE CAN ALL READ, GROW, CHANGE AND LEARN.

Are you wondering how you got to this point and where to go from here? One of my all-time favorite books is written by Andy Stanley. It's called, *The Principle of the Path: How to Get from Where You Are to Where You Want to Be.*

One of the book reviews about *Principle of the Path* had this to say about it:

> It is foolish for a person to seriously believe that all knowledge is already in his possession. Good decisions are made when you have tapped into as much knowledge and advice you can get, and submit to it.

Better Human and this chapter's mission are to get you to realize – honestly – where you currently are in life . Then, help you, push you, and **challenge you to be better.**

BY CHANGING, NOTHING NOTHING CHANGES.

— TONY ROBBINS

I am asking you to change. Bottom line.

I am asking you to get over yourself.

It's a matter of your choices, your attitude, and your actions. Always has been, always will be.

We all have negativity, challenges, opportunities and the same amount of time.

Think about the three S's that should rule over your life. During a chance encounter at Christmas, I heard the simplest of reminders as to how to live our lives and, more importantly, how to get over ourselves.

We have three things to do each day and every day that we are blessed with another breath:

WE ARE HERE TO **SHINE.**
WE ARE HERE TO **SERVE.**
WE ARE HERE TO **SHARE.**

Ask yourself in every thought and in all instances of your life if you are living up to the three S's.

AM I **SHINING**?

(I am positive, I am happy, I am grateful for all things.)

AM I **SERVING** OTHERS?

(I have left my self-absorbed world to help others,

which, in turn, helps me.)

AM I **SHARING**?

(I share myself, my love, my knowledge, and my resoureces

with all those I come in contact with.)

When you can answer YES to these three simple questions, you, my friend, **have gotten over yourself.**

"**You are a product of your environment.**
So choose the environment that will
best develop you toward your objective.
Analyze your life in term of its environment."

Are the things around you
HELPING you toward success —
or are they **HOLDING** you back?

— W. Clement Stone

CHAPTER SIX
WHAT ARE YOU PUTTING IN YOUR **KOOL-AID?**

In one of my sales meetings a few years back, I invited a friend to come share what he does with my team. He arrived early and was able to sit in for the first 30 minutes of our meeting. He was shocked. His company meetings were painful. Boring, long, no one spoke except for the head guy, people were on their phones or checking Twitter, basically doing anything but the meeting.

His first question after the meeting to me was: "What are you putting in their Kool-Aid?" He was certain I was slipping something in their morning brew. How did a room of people get so pumped up? Excited? Engaged?

I have long believed that it is my job as a leader to set the tone, fire the team up, be sure to surround them with opportunities to grow and make them feel like they can move mountains, have a voice, get a little crazy and, of course, have a flat good time.

Another visitor had the feedback that visiting my office and crew was like attending a rock concert. Music is pumping, people are moving at a high speed, success is in the air, and people are actually laughing and having fun at work.

Clement Stone asks one of the most important questions: "Are the things around you helping you toward success or holding you back?"

I work hard every day to protect my environment and take great care to know what I put in my Kool-Aid. There are key things that contribute to the Kool-Aid you drink and make up your life. I'm excited to share how I protect my attitude, my actions, and my choices.

GET A PEN OR PENCIL OUT.
WE HAVE SOME

WORK TO DO

WHO ARE YOUR **PEOPLE?**

Who are the top five people in your life with whom you
spend the most time?

1.

2.

3.

4.

5.

Write them down and then ask yourself, "Is that **good** news?" Do they fill your tank? Are they positive? Are they getting you farther from or closer to your goals? Do they love you? Do they make you want to be better? Do they help push you to be better?

At times in all of our lives, we have to clean house. I have been around the type of people who tear you down, hate you, and pretend to love you or have your best interest at heart. At the young age of 18, I realized I get to choose who I associate with no matter if they are family or friends. I have evicted friends and family out of my life as needed to be able to answer yes to all those questions above. Clean house. Find the ones that will help you achieve the life you deserve.

WHAT IS ON YOUR SCREEN?

What are you watching?
List the top five.

1.

2.

3.

4.

5.

Write them down and then ask yourself, "Is that **good** news?" Do the shows fill your tank? Are they positive? Are they getting you farther from or closer to your goals? Do they make you want to be better? Do they help push you to be better?

If you are spending your days and/or nights in front of the television watching mind-numbing shows (you know the ones), I beg you to stop now or at least cut back. Put yourself on a new strategy that says for every mind-cell sucking show you watch, you will watch something that pushes you to be more. You'll watch a Ted Talk or something on the Discovery Channel, or the History Channel.

I am a HUGE ESPN and sports fan. You won't find me in front of a television unless a sporting event is on and/or it is the weekend and I am treating myself to a movie. What you watch, you become. Make-over your watch list. Change your life.

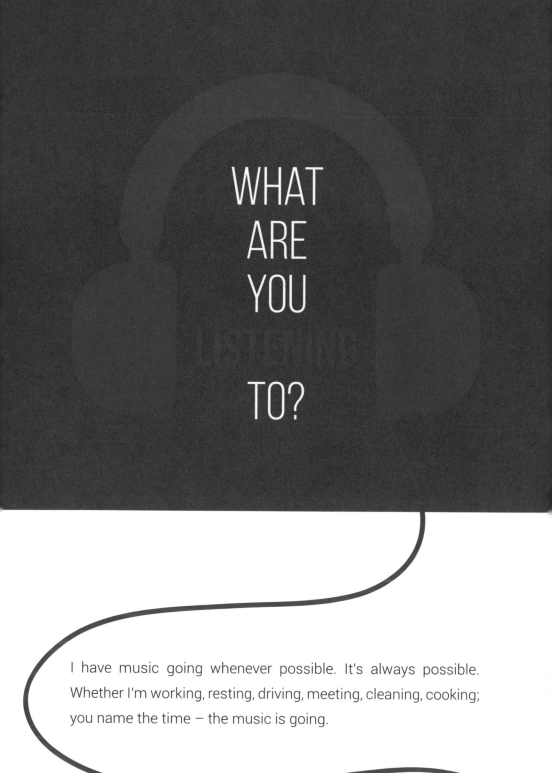

WHAT ARE YOU LISTENING TO?

I have music going whenever possible. It's always possible. Whether I'm working, resting, driving, meeting, cleaning, cooking; you name the time – the music is going.

I recently read an article called the *Surprising Effects of Music.*
Here are the cliff notes on the surprising effects music has on us:

IT...

- CAN HELP HEAL US.

- ENHANCES OUR LEARNING AND INTELLIGENCE.

- IMPROVES OUR PHYSICAL PERFORMANCE.

- IMPROVES OUR PRODUCTIVITY WHEN WE ARE LISTENING.

- HELPS TO CALM, RELAX AND GET YOU TO SLEEP.

- IMPROVES MOOD AND DECREASES DEPRESSION.

READ THIS betterhuman.today/pages/**music**

Did you read the benefits above? Surround yourself with music.
The right music. My interests are wide and vast. I have shared
one of my playlists with you. Turn it up and get ready for a rock
concert.

DOWNLOAD THIS FREEBIE PLEASE SHARE BY ALL MEANS.

www.spotify/betterhuman

WHAT ARE YOU READING?

This is a passionate topic for me. I have strong emotions about reading and what it does for you and your life. Reading has been an escape for me ever since I was a young child. I wanted a life different than mine. I would read and escape. It showed me that life was **BIG** and there was so much to do.

Now, I realize that reading is a game changer. I read all day. I read every day.

I read an unfathomable number of blogs, quotes, tweets, magazines, books, and websites. My husband swears my head may pop off based on over consumption.

Let's do a quick reading audit.

DO YOU READ **DAILY**?

HOW MANY BOOKS **A MONTH** DO YOU READ?

WHAT TYPES OF **BLOGS** ARE YOU READING?

DO YOU **SUBSCRIBE** TO MONTHLY MAGAZINES?

Write them down and then ask yourself — am I doing enough? Can I be better? What can I add? What would get me closer to the life I envision?

Do you need help knowing where to begin? I track all of my favorite books on **betterhuman.today/pages/books**. Start there.

I subscribe to the following magazines:

Success
Experience Life
Forbes
Fast Company
Entrepreneur
Sports Illustrated
Builder
Professional Builder
Inc.

Do you see the pattern? I read only things that align with my goals. Yes, I read *People* magazine or some fabulous fiction books from time to time when I am flying or when I need an escape once in a while. I focus on making sure that 80 percent of my reading materials are focused on the right things. The important things. Things that will help me grow.

WHAT ARE YOU DOING?

If I asked you how your days are spent how would break it down?

READ THIS / betterhuman.today/pages/**spendyourdays**

Go to the link above and it will tell you IN LIVE time what America is doing. It's crazy. Seriously go.

When I last looked, eighty four million Americans were watching television. Six million were playing *Call of Duty*. Three million were learning. Okay so it didn't really say *Call of Duty* but it did show a video game console. I assumed.

DO AN AUDIT OF YOUR DAYS.

List the five main activities in your life.

1.

2.

3.

4.

5.

Write them down and then ask yourself, "Is that **good** news?" Do they fill your tank? Are they positive? Are they getting you farther from or closer to your goals? Do they make you want to be better? Do they help push you to be better?

My five are always a WIP (work in progress).

1. MEDITATE

2. FAMILY

3. WORK

4. READ

5. FUEL (SLEEP, EAT, WORKOUT)

PLAN YOUR DAYS. PLAN YOUR LIFE. DON'T BE SURPRISED BY HOW YOU SPEND YOUR HOURS. THEY ARE **YOUR** HOURS.

Again, I ask you, "Are you a Pilot or a Passenger?"

Well, which is it? Are you guiding your life as a Pilot or sitting in the Passenger seat hoping to God it goes well for you. The Passenger who has no direction, no choice, no thought, no effort, no goals – is not the look we are going for.

Nine years ago I read a book called *The Good Life Rules* by Bryan Dodge. He is the reason I started my QFD (Quote for the Day). He suggested in his book that I start my day and the day of those around me with one positive quote or thought. To change my thinking. I did it. This year I decided to change the name of the quote to **Better Thinking**.

I was asked once what the quote means and why I do it every day?

The Good Life Rules by Bryan Dodge

It was first and foremost to help with my thinking. I wanted to think better. I wanted something every day to start my day in a positive manner. All part of the Kool-Aid. I started to grow my list: I added my team, family, and friends and then started adding the people who attended my speaking engagements. Then it grew to contain wives, husbands, sons, daughters, mothers, of those already receiving my Better Thinking quote.

Sign up for Better Thinking at

www.BetterHuman.today

DRiVE The Surprising Truth
About What Motivates Us Daniel Pink

DRiVE

BE GRATE

DO ALL
THINGS
WITH
LOVE

I follow several people each day to help push me. I can't wait to open my Twitter feed and my inbox to find their daily message. Here are a few of my favorites:

TUT Notes from the Universe

Givemore.com

Leadercast

Huffington Post

Life Hacks

Third Metric

Michael Hyatt

Dr. Henry Cloud

Jon Acuff

My office is a place I spend a LARGE amount of time in. I want to share with you what I look at all day...

WHAT KIND OF *Kool-aid* IS HANGING ON MY WALLS.

By now, hopefully, you have looked at every area of your life and have a plan as to what needs to be changed, added, deleted, and tweaked. Don't leave any area of your life unexamined.

So, one more time, I ask...

"WHAT ARE YOU PUTTING

IN YOUR
KOOL-AID?"

"EVERYONE IS HANDED ADVERSITY IN LIFE. NO ONE'S JOURNEY IS EASY. **IT'S HOW THEY HANDLE IT THAT MAKES PEOPLE UNIQUE.**"

— KEVIN CONROY

CHAPTER SEVEN
IF YOU'RE HANDED IT, YOU CAN HANDLE IT.

Whatever has been handed to you is in your life for a purpose. I have lived and thrived by the motto: If you're handed it, you can handle it. We all have our own journey. It is not easy all of the time, nor is it filled with rainbows and unicorns.

When a parent dies suddenly and unexpectedly you are filled with mass confusion. There has been a mistake. This can't be right. Why me? Why now?

My mother died in a car accident when I was 3 years old. My siblings were 10 and 13. I've heard so many different viewpoints on this over the years. Some would say I was the lucky one because I was too little to remember. My siblings had it tougher because they did have time and memories with our mother.

 This is messed up. But we are handed it, so we handle it. I focus on the fact that I had three years, that I was born, that she gave me the gift of life. I focus on the chance to make her proud each day.

I will not feel slighted or wronged. My husband firmly believes that I am the strong person I am today because of it. I look for the gift. I look for the positive. If I do not the, potential of sorrow, grief, and pity will take over my life.

That will never do.

What are you feeling slighted or wronged about in your life right now? Write it down.

Turn it. Look for the lesson. Look for the gift.
Remember my story about Henry, the Bible Scholar? The man was robbed. He turned it into a gift, into thankfulness.

I recently heard Leon Rice, the head coach of the Boise State University men's basketball program, speak. His team must ask themselves in every instance: Are you a Victim or a Warrior? He spoke about choosing to be accountable for your life, your decisions, and your actions.

You are right, things do happen to you. What you decide after that is all within your control. Every f-bomb, every eye roll, every tear, every bout of sadness, anger, anxiety, worry and more, are all up to you.

WHAT HAVE YOU BEEN **HANDED**?
ARE YOU HANDLING IT?
OR IS IT HANDLING YOU?

ARE YOU **A VICTIM**
OR **A WARRIOR?**

A VICTIM ASKS, "**WHY ME?**" IT SAYS, "**I DON'T DESERVE THIS.**"

THE WARRIOR SAYS, "I CAN HANDLE IT. I CAN BE BETTER BECAUSE OF THIS." WARRIORS SAY THANK YOU.

One of my favorite lessons of all times is: life is not fair. It is lopsided, biased, giving in some areas, lacking in others. There is no balance or righteousness or sense.

My nanny always said, "You get what you get and you don't throw a fit." This quote has served me well in life. From age three until now.

Write down a **negative memory** and find the **positives.**

Then think of a **success** and find the **positives.**

Joel Osteen is the author of one of my favorite books, *You Can You Will*. Chapter four is titled, "Have a Positive Mindset." He talks about how we choose our mindset each day. No one can force you to have a certain mindset. Not your spouse, your boss, your parents, your siblings or your friends.

You decide every day.

Choose the right one.

Start your day with the right mindset, he says. When you wake up choose to be happy, to be grateful.

A NEGATIVE ATTITUDE WILL LIMIT YOUR LIFE.

REPEAT THAT SENTENCE.

A NEGATIVE ATTITUDE WILL LIMIT YOUR LIFE.

Fewer opportunities, less success, less love, fewer friends.

Choose the right thoughts no matter the circumstances. There is good and bad in every situation.

Choose the good. Choose to be happy right where you are.

You control how happy you want to be.

When my second son was born four weeks early, it was a wild ride. The birth of my first son was an uneventful healthy, happy, cakewalk type of event. We were expecting more of the same.

My second son, by all rights, appeared healthy. Even though he came four weeks early, he still weighed in at a whopping 9 lbs. 8 oz. They wrapped him up, handed him to Dad, and said congrats!

My husband was blessed to hold our newborn son on the way up to his room. With a nurse by his side, my son stopped breathing and went blue about half way up. The nurse kept shouting to my husband, "Pinch him, smack the bottom of his feet." She pushed some magical button and the doors of the elevator opened and my husband swears some insane swat team was waiting as they grabbed our son and took off running, no less than a hundred of them, he says.

Yes, my boy was big but underdeveloped in the lung and digestion area. He went on to spend 19 days in the Neonatal Intensive Care Unit of the hospital. My husband and I would stay all day and most of the night. We only went home for about four hours each night to sleep. Six days into his stay, in the middle of the night, my son stopped breathing again. My husband and I had just left the hospital around 11 p.m. that evening. I woke that night at 2 a.m. and called the nurse's station next to my son's bassinet to ask them to check on him.

Nobody answered.

I then called the main reception of the hospital. They apologized and said they were sorry my nurse did not answer but my son had stopped breathing and they were trying to resuscitate him. My son was brought back to us that night and released two weeks later but not until we were trained in CPR and given a monitor that tracks when he stops breathing. It was a stressful first couple of months; he was sick, we were stressed and tired. All I could do was say thank you for this gift and keep pushing each day to get him healthier and stronger. At three months I thought we were turning a corner.

I was wrong.

I had just dropped off my oldest for pre-school and was back at home warming up a bottle. My son was in his bouncy chair, as I shook it and tested it, I was (of course) making faces and talking to my son.

He stopped breathing. He went blue. Right in front of me eyes. I grabbed him and my phone. I proceeded to start CPR. I called 911 on speaker while I cleared airways and gave breaths. I shouted to the operator, "My son has stopped breathing. Please send help." She then asked if I had started CPR, and how old he was. The one question she didn't ask was "what is your address?"

At that exact moment five or six off-duty firemen came barreling through my front door and grabbed my son from me. All I can remember is yelling to the operator "They're here. They're here!" She responded back "Who ma'am? Who?"

Those off duty fireman had their radio on and heard the call taking place. They were driving by my house at that exact moment on their way to training.

THEY SAVED MY SON'S LIFE.

It reminds me of a book called *When God Winks* by Squire Rushnell. God Winked that day. He sent those firement to me.

I am asked all the time how could I remain so calm, how did I give my three-month-old son CPR without losing my shit.

I was handed it and I handled it.

I wanted to win that day. I wanted to be a warrior for my son and myself. I was not interested in being a victim.

The book that I think about often when I am having first-world problems, like the line at Starbucks, or my email won't load fast enough, or the plane I'm flying on doesn't have Wi-Fi, is called *Man's Search for Meaning* by Viktor Frankl.

READ THIS / *Man's Search for Meaning* by Viktor Frankl

Man's Search for Meaning is a book written in 1946 by Viktor Frankl chronicling his experiences as an Auschwitz concentration camp inmate during World War II. According to a survey conducted by the Book-of-the-Month Club and the Library of Congress, *Man's Search For Meaning* belongs to a list of **"The ten most influential books in the United States."**

I share this book with you in hopes that it will help keep our lives in perspective. Frankl was an amazing man who came out of an horrific time and events with a heart filled with love and healing.

One of his famous quotes says it all,

"WHEN WE ARE NO LONGER ABLE TO CHANGE A SITUATION, WE ARE CHALLENGED TO CHANGE OURSELVES."

You are going to come across events, situations, crises that you are not able to change or control. I pray that you focus on what you can do.

You can find the good. You can handle it.

Part of finding the good in your life is choosing happiness. I have a question for you:

What is the most popular class at Harvard University?

Google this | What is the most popular class at Harvard?

The answer is:
Positive Psychology: How to be Happier.

Even Harvard students need help with their mindset. They, too, are learning to be happy, and are busy working on their mindsets.

Happiness is a skill not a trait. Here's the difference:

trait
/trāt/ *noun*

A genetically determined characteristic or condition.

skill
/skil/ *verb*

To practice. To do something well.

Here's what those definitions mean to me: You cannot say you were born an unhappy person. You are choosing it. You choose to practice negativity, you choose to be unhappy.

Now for the good news. You can practice happiness. You can change. Say thank you, smile, give love, hug someone, help someone, happily serve.

Happiness is a skill. **Seek out the happiness.**

This one skill will be the game changer when life gets rough.

IF YOU ARE HANDED IT, YOU CAN HANDLE IT.

"SURROUND YOURSELF WITH
GOOD THOUGHTS,
GOOD PEOPLE,
AND GOOD IDEAS
AND GOOD THINGS WILL HAPPEN."
– SAM PARKER

CHAPTER EIGHT

IT TAKES A **VILLAGE**

My father used to say to me as I was heading to school, "Hang with dogs, you are a dog." I couldn't agree more. I was perplexed at times when he seemed to have quite a few "dogs" around him. Then came my other favorite quote: "Do as I say, not as I do."

Well said.

My life has been made up of some amazing people. It has taken a village to get me where I am in this life. I am forever grateful.

We can only go so far on our own. We need people who lift us up, give us hope, love us unconditionally. This chapter is about examining your current village, carefully creating your village, auditing your village and saying thank you to those people who fill your tank.

First things first. We discussed earlier in the book the five people you spend the most time with. They are a HUGE part of your village. I ask you again, do these five people fill up your tank? Are they a positive influence on your life? Do they support your dreams? Do they love you?

If you can't answer yes, then it is time to clean house. I have no tolerance for people in my life who do not fuel my tank, love me, respect me and share in my excitement about what life holds. I have been called ruthless before. So be it. When you lower your standards you are setting yourself up for failure.

"LIFE IS AN ELEVATOR,

ON YOUR WAY UP SOMETIMES YOU HAVE TO STOP AND LET SOME PEOPLE OFF."

— AUTHOR UNKNOWN

Jim Rohn said it best: "You are the average of the five people you spend the most time with." How's your average? Who's bringing down your average? Are you showing gratitude for those who keep your average up?

Choose your village wisely. My village growing up was an unconventional crew. Even at a young age I understood the importance of seeking out the good. My dearest childhood friend and her parents were part of that crew. They helped me realize that your village can come in all shapes and sizes. They took care of me, loved me and showed me a different way of life. My first step mother came into my life when I was four years old and has never left. My father divorced her when I was seven. By all rights, she should have walked away. She didn't. She swears my mother sent her to me and I believe her. She never gave up on me. All these years she has been in my corner cheering for me, pushing me and loving me.

This is what I hope for you. These types of people.
Seek them out.

I had other people in my life that did the exact opposite, they hated me, they tore me down, told me I was less than nothing. I evicted them as soon as I could. I urge you to do the same.

WE DON'T HAVE TIME FOR **HATE, ANGER** OR **JEALOUSY.**

DON'T JUSTIFY IT
or try to
UNDERSTAND IT.

In Tom Rath's book *How Full Is Your Bucket?* he notes that it takes five positive interactions to get rid of one negative interaction. **WOW.** If you are allowing negative people in your life, in your village, you are promising yourself an uphill climb.

If you hang with dogs, you will become a dog. You will start behaving like them, talking like them, watching, doing and listening to all the same things. Why do we urge our children to pick their friends so carefully while we, ourselves, do a horrible job of it?

THE CHOICE IS YOURS.

CHOOSE WISELY.

BE PICKY.

I work with an amazing village. I love all of them. Can you say that about your career? Your job? The people you work with? You should. You spend a HUGE amount of time with your co-workers, your teammates. Make sure it's the right village. My personal cheerleader and director of all things sassy have been in my life for more than 16 years. These are people who fuel my tank, who love me and who have helped me get where I am today. I make sure I love them accordingly with lunches, surprise coffee runs, thank you cards, and more.

MY FAMILY'S RAP NAME IS CFOUR, for the four Congers. It's made up of me, my

husband of 25 years, and my two teenage sons. We are incredibly close. We work on it everyday. We text, call, FaceTime, email and share everything. We celebrate each other's lives, we push and encourage accordingly. You have to take great care of your village. We say "love you" at every opportunity. When I speak to large groups, right before I go on stage I look down at my phone one last time knowing that my oldest son will have sent me a text right before each event telling me he loves me and that I am going to kill it.

My husband believes that he should never stop courting. He sends me flowers often, he stops by my office out of the blue to say he loves me, he sends me text messages throughout the day telling me I look hot. And I reciprocate. I leave love letters in his car, text messages throughout the day. All of these are things that keep my village thriving, happy and connected. I hope that you will do the same.

This book and my website www.betterhuman.today never would have happened without my village. We call that village the Better Human Energy Crew. Writing a book, creating a movement, a lifestyle called **BETTER** HUMAN has been on my list for years. I have dreamed about it, prayed about it and wanted it with all my heart.

Last summer I realized that the only way it would ever happen is if I had help. It was going to take a village. I approached four amazing women who I knew had some insane talents. They said, "HELL, YES," when I asked them to help me make Better Human a reality. I am forever grateful.

INSPECT ALL AREAS OF YOUR LIFE. **LEAVE *NOTHING* TO CHANCE.**

If you are currently surrounded by a fabulous village, please do two things for me. First, I would like you to thank them, send them a HANDWRITTEN letter (please no texts or emails). Tell them how important they are to you and that you appreciate all they do for you.

The second thing I want you to do is hug it out. Yup, you read that correctly. I want you to find all those in your village, whether it be at home, at work, at school, at church, or at Starbucks. Then, as I noted in Chapter One, I want you to **hug it out.**

HUG IT OUT.

Earlier, I mentioned Leon Rice, the head coach of the Boise State University Men's Basketball team. He shared a fascinating study called *Study: Good Players Aren't Afraid To Touch Teammates* by Henry Abbott of ESPN.com. Here's an excerpt from the article:

" Michael W. Kraus led a research team that coded every bump, hug and high five in a single game played by each team in the National Basketball Association early last season.

In a paper due out this year in the journal *Emotion*, Mr. Kraus and his co-authors, Cassy Huang and Dr. Dacher Keltner, report that with a few exceptions, good teams tended to be touchier than bad ones. The most touch-bonded teams were the Boston Celtics and the Los Angeles Lakers, currently two of the league's top teams; at the bottom were the mediocre Sacramento Kings and Charlotte Bobcats.

The same was true, more or less, for players. The touchiest player was Kevin Garnett, the Celtics' star big man, followed by star forwards Chris Bosh of the Toronto Raptors and Carlos Boozer of the Utah Jazz. 'Within 600 milliseconds of shooting a free throw, Garnett has reached out and touched four guys,' Dr. Keltner said. **"**

I fell in love with this article and the idea behind it. I share it with you to show the importance of how you interact and love your village. This affects all areas of your life. Do not take anything for granted. We need to know we are loved, appreciated and, more importantly, we need to be hugged.

Are you hugging it out? Giving high fives? Fist pumps and more?

You should be.

Boost others' confidence, show them love, get them fired up.

Create the right village.

LOVE YOUR VILLAGE.

"KEEP **RAISING** YOUR EXPECTATIONS.

UP LET'S EVERYTHING."

– Jon Gruden

CHAPTER NINE

MUCH HAS BEEN **GIVEN,** MUCH IS **EXPECTED**

You're breathing.

You're alive.

Much has been **given** to you.

Much is **expected**.

Enough said.

I so wanted those first couple of sentences to be the entire chapter. Read them again. That is **DEEP**. Are you with me? Let me spell it out for you.

If you are alive right here, right now, then much has been given to you AND much will be expected.

You are here for a reason. You have work to do.

YOU MUST GET IT ALL. Do not take one second for granted.

I love people, I am one of those people who meets someone new and falls in love with all of the incredible possibilities I see in them.

A couple of years ago I took a test. From Tom Rath's book, *Strength Finders 2.0*, I learned my top five strengths, a couple of which are Maximizer and Strategic. I want to maximize, get the most out of EVERYTHING and then, of course, make sure they are in the right place.

Have you taken the *Strength Finder 2.0* test yet? It's one of the best ways to learn about yourself and what your strengths are and how to use them.

READ THIS — *Strengths Finder 2.0* by Tom Rath

You need to know your strengths so you use them accordingly. We are not here to get by or go through the motions. If I wasn't such a wus I would make all of us get tattoos that said **GET IT ALL.**

Much has been given. Much is expected. I say this over and over each day so I remember to take nothing for granted. I stay focused on the task at hand. I work on being a better human, doing more, giving to those around me, serving happily and loving this life.

How about you? Have you said thank you today for this life? Hanging in my office is one of my all-time favorite canvases. I see it every morning and it keeps me focused.
Welcome to my fabulous life state of mind.

IF YOU ARE BREATHING, LIFE IS FABULOUS. BOTTOM LINE.

I WAKE UP EACH MORNING BESIDE MYSELF WITH JOY THAT I GET ANOTHER CHANCE TO GIVE AS MUCH AS I CAN.

Seth Godin, or **the word magician** (as I like to call him), recently published the most beautiful book: *What To Do When It's Your Turn (and It's Always Your Turn).* He talks about digging deep. Doing the work that scares you, or pushes you outside your comfort zone.

Writing this book was definitely outside my wheelhouse. I love to speak to groups, I love meeting with people one on one. I'm animated, intensely passionate and strut around the stage like a crazy chicken during my presentations. Writing has been a new challenge for me. I am learning to love it and decided that by doing this book it falls in line with my belief that much has been given, so much will be expected of me.

I speak at least once a month or more to a wide range of people and companies. At least one person per event will ask me how they can buy my book.

About five years ago I was speaking to a large group. At the end I had a man come up to me and hand me his business card. He told me he would like to buy a copy of my book. I said, "Sorry for the confusion, but I have not written a book." He said, "You will and when you do please email me. I would like to buy a copy."

Sometimes we need others to show us or remind us what is possible. To remind us to dig deep. Jon Gruden got it right when he said, "Keep raising your expectations. Let's up everything."

WHAT HAVE YOU BEEN TOLD THAT YOU ARE GOOD AT?

WHAT DO YOU DREAM ABOUT?

GO THERE. DO THAT.

I can hardly wait to see what you will do. Feel free to drop me a line and share your greatness: **ronda@betterhuman.today**

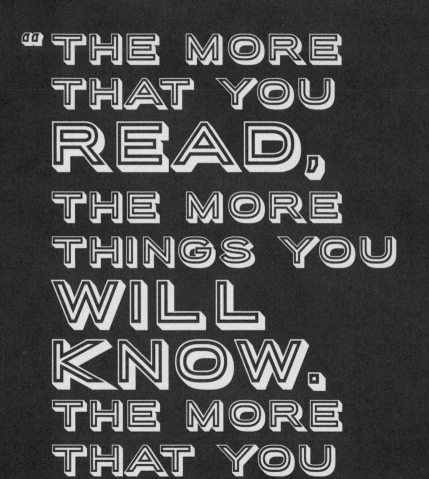

"THE MORE
THAT YOU
READ,
THE MORE
THINGS YOU
WILL
KNOW.
THE MORE
THAT YOU

CHAPTER TEN
SCHOOL IS **NOT** OUT

Darren Hardy the editor of *SUCCESS* Magazine has spent his career interviewing thousands of the top CEOs, business owners, professional athletes and more. He decided after years of interviewing these highly successfully people to find a common thread. What did they all share? What did they all do on a regular basis that anyone could do?

They read up to five books per week. Yes, per week. They are on an endless pursuit of knowledge. These people are at the TOP of their games and they fully realize that school is not out.

Every year Bill Gates takes a two week reading vacation?

Shut up.

He goes away with a stack of books and reads. For two weeks. He understands the importance of learning, growing and pushing forward.

Jim Rohn says it best:

IF YOU WANT TO HAVE MORE,
YOU HAVE TO BECOME MORE.

FOR THINGS TO IMPROVE,
YOU HAVE TO IMPROVE.

FOR THINGS TO GET BETTER,
YOU HAVE TO GET BETTER.

FOR THINGS TO CHANGE,
YOU HAVE TO CHANGE.

WHEN YOU CHANGE,
EVERYTHING CHANGES FOR YOU.

People talk about their less than stellar lives, their wants, their hopes. But then sit there and do **nothing about it**. Here's my challenge for you today:

WRITE DOWN **ONE THING** YOU WANT/DREAM/WISH ABOUT:

Google what you wrote down.

Search for a book, a video, an article about your dream.

Read it.

You are now one step closer to realizing your dream. Keep Googling, learning, researching until you have the tools to make your dreams come true. The key words in that sentence are **YOU HAVE THE TOOLS TO MAKE YOUR DREAMS COME TRUE.**

Stop waiting.

Stop wishing.

Start doing. THE BELL **HAS** RUNG. *School* **IS IN!**

Rumor has it that some people find reading daunting, overwhelming and, at times, boring. That just means that they are doing it all wrong. First things first, search out only those materials that you are passionate about and that get you one step closer to your dreams.

TINY HABITS

Second, let's start with a tiny habit. I love tiny habits. Dr. B.J. Fogg came up with the idea and it has spread across the globe on every level imaginable. From flossing your teeth, to doing push ups, to reading and so much more. Get your Google on and check it out.

The tiny habit I want to talk about is reading.

What if I told you I could forever change your life if you gave me four minutes per day? You can improve your life with just four minutes per day.

Would you give me four minutes? Just say **yes.**

Let's start with something small and impactful. If you were to purchase John Maxwell's book *Today Matters* and you read four minutes a day, you would be done in one months' time. **TRY IT.** Better yet, pick up a copy of the book for yourself and also for someone you know who needs to change/improve his life.

Ted Talks have changed the world. They have brought some of the most thrilling, imaginative, educational, thought provoking, never-before-accessed information to the masses. I will be forever grateful. I feel like Harvard's got nothing on me.

www.betterhuman.today/pages/**tedtalks**

Watch one video. Bet you can't stop with just one.

Ignorance is no longer bliss. You have the resources to improve your life. You just have to get to it. Put the remote down. Turn the boob tube off and go learn something already.

If I was to give you a
LEARNING BLUEPRINT
it would go something like this:

GOOGLE
a topic you are passionate about.

FIND BLOGS that relate to
that subject and follow them!

READ their blogs on a **regular basis.**

Now go to Amazon or another friendly book seller and
FIND A BOOK.

READ it **4 MINUTES** a day!

Visit Ted Talks once a week.
Pick one video that **inspires** you and **WATCH IT.**

Pick a magazine that speaks to you
and **your dream.**
SUBSCRIBE TO IT.

Search for webinars and/or conferences.
GO THERE.

BE A PILOT.
CHART YOUR PATH
AND GET TO IT.

YOUR DREAM IS
WAITING.

At the beginning of each year I put together my growth plan for the year. Here's what is on my list for 2015:

I will attend four big conferences:

Two Career Related and Two Personal Growth Related. The Pacific Coast Builders Conference in San Diego and the International Builder Show in Las Vegas. Leadercast in Atlanta and Tony Robbins in Chicago.

I subscribe to no less than 20 blogs on a variety of topics.

Magazine subscriptions to: *Fast Company, Entrepreneur, Experience Life, Forbes* and *SUCCESS*.

I keep a book list for the year, tracking all the books I've read.

Don't leave it up to chance or hope. Plan your growth. Plan your life.

School is in.

CHARLIE TREMENDOUS JONES SAYS THAT
YOU WILL BE THE
SAME PERSON
IN FIVE YEARS
AS YOU ARE TODAY
EXCEPT
FOR THE
PEOPLE YOU MEET
AND THE
BOOKS YOU READ.

My nightstand overfloweth with books. Sweet, **glorious** books. I will be forever curious on this thing we call life and all things related. My desire for better is strong. I realize if I want better I have to work for it. I have to read, explore, challenge my old thinking and push myself.

Here are 10 of my favorite books:

Aspire by Kevin Hall

Smile and Move by Sam Parker

20,000 Days and Counting by Robert D. Smith

The Principle of the Path by Andy Stanley

The Traveler's Gift by Andy Andrews

The Little Red Book of Wisdom by Mark DeMoss

177 Mental Toughness Secrets of the World Class by Steve Siebold

A Short Guide to a Happy Life by Anna Quindlen

Man's Search for Meaning by Viktor E. Frankl

Thrive by Arianna Huffington

The definition of GROW is to become greater over a period of time; increase. I encourage you to grow in all areas. If you are lacking in an area then study that area. I read about marriage, parenting, leadership, health, spiritual and more. Twenty-five years of marriage takes growth, knowledge and work. Parenting is a full-time and eyes-wide-open type of adventure. Leading myself and my teams takes everything I've got. I study for myself and then share with all those I come in contact.

One of my favorite West African Proverbs says this:

A MAN WHO DOES NOT LEAVE HIS HUT WILL BRING **NOTHING IN.**

Go to conferences, go to the bookstore, go to the library, watch a Ted Talk. Leave your hut and bring back knowledge, wisdom, experience and watch your world expand.

I hear people tell me that they will never read or go to a class again. High school and college were more than enough for them. I low sad. This is when life gets good. You get to choose what you watch, read and experience. You get to learn about new passions, new dreams, and new adventures. Good for you if you completed school in a traditional sense.

Don't stop now.

School is NoT out.
It's just getting interesting...

EVERYTHING IS POSSIBLE

FOR ONE WHO **BELIEVES.**

- Mark 9:23

CHAPTER ELEVEN
DREAM **BIG**, PRAY **BIG**

Hold on to your knickers. We are going to have some fun. Dreaming and praying. Two of my favorites. I firmly believe that today I am living the life I dreamed of and prayed for.

How about you? Can you say the same?

Are you dreaming **BIG?** Praying **BIG?**

Small minds create small lives. You were not meant for a small life. I can guarantee you that.

Let's get to work.

WRITE DOWN 3 GOALS/DREAMS YOU WANT **RIGHT NOW**.

1.

2.

3.

Now pull out your cell phone, open your calendar and answer this question:

DOES YOUR DAY REFLECT YOUR GOALS?

Your calendar should have appointments and to-do lists each day that get you closer to your goals. I went to lunch with a friend in the real estate industry and she said to me, "I want to be a top producer in real estate, but it's not working." I asked her to hand me her cell phone. I opened up her calendar and what I saw shocked me. She had her yoga appointments on her calendar but nothing else. I said to her "Not so sure your real estate dreams have a shot at the current moment but a career in yoga looks promising based on the number of times you go each week."

Her calendar should have been filled with appointments and time blocks of calling for referrals, sending out mailers, holding open houses, visiting past sellers and so on.

You cannot be surprised about not hitting your goals if you are not making them a priority each day.

PLAN YOUR DAYS. PLAN YOUR LIFE.

Right now, take a look and see what your day says about you.

Add a time on your calendar this week for an action that gets you closer to your dreams.

Hold yourself accountable. Put it on your calendar to keep it top of mind. Create days that are focused and purposeful. Stop wandering and wishing.

A few years ago I was speaking at a local chamber event. Before I went on stage to present a young man spoke of his time as a volunteer for a local bike race in town and was sharing details as to how others could volunteer. Little did I know that he was not truly a member of the Chamber. He was there only to discuss the race and then planned to leave. When he was finished I jumped up and spoke on one of my favorite topics, "What Are You Putting in Your Kool-Aid?"

He ended up staying for my whole presentation. I had no idea. I spoke about the importance of what we speak over our lives. The law of expectations. If you think negative thoughts, you should not be surprised when you get negative in return. If you knew how powerful your thoughts really are, you would never think a negative thought again. I explained the need to keep your expectations and thinking in a positive manner which is in line with your dreams and hopes. I also had that group write down one goal on a card. I asked them to be **bold** about it, pray about it, expect the positive, put all energies toward it.

If you realized how powerful your **thoughts are**

you would never think
a negative thought.

– Peace Pilgrim

One month later I received an email from the young man. He explained to me that he truly wasn't supposed to stay that day or listen to me speak. He went on to say that he was in a bad place in his life. He had been unemployed for two years and his attitude was in a terrible place about life or ever finding a job. He thanked me for changing his life that day. He wrote down his employment goal on his card and changed his thinking. He reported that he was now employed and forever grateful. He went on to ask me to speak to a group of unemployed men that he had been meeting with for the last six months. He wanted to help them as well.

Your thoughts, the things you dream about, write down and focus on have unbelievable powers. I am so proud of that young man and the thing I love most is that he paid it forward.

READ THIS / *Think Big* by Robert Anthony

Every morning I wake up and I say thank you for another day. I then go through my whole day and everyone in it. I pray for all of it. I bless everyone that I am going to come in contact with.

I pray big. I pray all day. Before every meeting, every call, every interaction.

And then at night I do it a little differently.

I say thank you for the day and then I pray for all those in my life and the day ahead.

If for some reason the word *pray* freaks you out, then choose another word that works for you. Just be sure you are putting good thoughts and powerful expectations over your life. Always.

MY LIFE IS NOTHING BUT A DREAM. MY DREAMS.

I have a vision board, a bucket list, yearly goals and a growth plan that guide my actions, attitude and results. We get but one ride on this ferris wheel and we better make it count.

When you do all those things you are placing your order. You are calling forward all the things that will help you obtain your dreams.

Create your bucket list.
List all the things you want to see, do and achieve.
Now place it on your bathroom mirror.

DREAM **BIG** MY FRIENDS. NOTHING ELSE WILL DO.

PRAY **BIG**. YOU NEED TO BELIEVE.

REMEMBER,
ANYTHING IS
POSSIBLE FOR
THE ONE WHO
BELIEVES.

YOU THINK BIG.

YOU
GET
BIG.

— THE NOTORIOUS B.I.G.

70% OF SUCCESS IN LIFE IS SHOWING UP

– WOODY ALLEN

CHAPTER TWELVE
IT'S **SHOWTIME,** BABY

I will never forget my first sales meeting with KB Homes in Las Vegas roughly 20 years ago. The President of the division, Jay Moss, came in for the last five minutes to inspire the sales team for the upcoming weekend.

He told a story about the performers of the Broadway musical *The Phantom of the Opera*. Every night the curtain goes up and **IT'S SHOWTIME, BABY**. He said it with such passion, such gusto, with zest, with enthusiasm. He likened the curtain dropping with our careers and our lives. No one would have a clue that the actors and actresses have had a bad day, that they fought with their spouses or that their dog had died. Once the curtain goes up, they are professionals, they are ready, they leave their problems and woes behind them.

They are dressed to the nines, they look beautiful in their freshly pressed costumes, their makeup is flawless, and their hair is freshly coiffed (I've always wanted to use that word). They are ready to give their best to the day, to the performance.

It's Showtime, Baby.

I have carried this lesson with me ever since. People do not want to know the miseries of your day or your life. We are not meant to wander through days sharing our grievances with any and all we come in contact with.

WE ARE HERE TO SHINE AND SOMETIMES THAT IS GOING TO BE HARD.

REAL HARD.

SOME PEOPLE BRIGHTEN A ROOM WHEN THEY WALK IN. OTHERS WHEN THEY WALK OUT.

WHICH ONE ARE YOU?

— COURTESY OF CHRIS WIDENER

My Nanny growing up always said to me

"Pretty is as pretty does."

Took me forever to realize what she was talking about. I finally get it.

I will only be as pretty as my actions and thoughts.

There are so many times we are on stage and that we need to be present and give our all.

In our careers, our jobs, our marriages, with our children, at the grocery story, at a coffee shop and so on. It appears at times we have given up the fight. We are in sweatpants, with hair that hasn't been washed for days, void of makeup and hiding under baseball caps.

I have two theories that go along with Showtime:

LOOK LIKE A MILLION BUCKS.
MAKE A MILLION BUCKS.

YOU CAN NEVER BE OVERDRESSED OR OVEREDUCATED.

I am shocked when interviewees show up for a job interview in jeans. When people are working in a professional setting in Juicy sweatpants or walking around in flip flops. How can we take you seriously? When you, yourself, seem so careless about you and the way you present yourself?

On more than one occasion in the last six months, I have been in a coffee shop and a grocery store in the middle of the day picking up supplies for work. On both occurrences the cashier commented on how beautiful I looked and wanted to know what the special occasion was.

The special occasion was work.

I was working.

How are you presenting yourself? How much care are you putting into you?

As Jon Gruden says, "Let's UP everything." Your wardrobe, your hair, your attitude, your knowledge, your choices.

IT'S SHOW TIME, BABY.

YOU'VE GOT
WHAT IT TAKES.
BUT IT WILL TAKE
EVERYTHING
YOU'VE GOT.
-AUTHOR UNKNOWN

CHAPTER THIRTEEN
BE **ALL IN**

Life is a boomerang. What you give, you get. If you want your life to be full, then you have to give it everything you've got.

Nothing else will do.

YOU WANT AN **AMAZING MARRIAGE**?

You have to give it 100 percent. Today the current divorce rate is at 50 percent. It's because people are only giving 50 percent of their attention, love and care to it.

YOU WANT A CAREER WHERE YOU ARE **THRIVING** AND **SUCCESSFUL**?

Stop punching the clock, stop doing the minimum, stop looking for better jobs and get busy making your current choice amazing. Start early, go long, work hard, work like you own the joint, become an expert.

YOU WANT **BETTER KIDS**?

Spend time with them. Listen to them. Love them. Be present in their lives. Be a role model worth following.

You choose your level of commitment to your life and the things in it through your actions, attitude and results.

BE ALL IN. WE NEED YOU.

Write this question on your bathroom
mirror with a marker:

AM I BEING
THE BEST
THAT I CAN BE?

Time to pick up your game. I recently read the book *20,000 Days and Counting* by Robert D. Smith. What a healthy perspective on making your days count.

He says this about the choices in your life:

"Despite all the realms of choicelessness, we do choose how we will live."

Be clear. Your life is made up of your choices.

Want different? Choose different.

Want more? Do more.

Want better? For things to get better, you have to get better.

I watched a Ted Talk recently that asked the question:

WHAT IS THE KEY TO SUCCESS?

WATCH THIS

www.betterhuman.today/pages/**grit**

IT'S NOT ~~TALENT.~~

IT'S NOT ~~IQ.~~

IT'S NOT ~~WEALTH.~~

IT'S **GRIT.**

TIME TO DIG DEEP.

CALL FORTH THE WARRIOR.

BECOME A PILOT.

LET'S DO THIS.

The beauty of life is that you get to start each day **anew**. Each day, you get to awaken to the opportunity to find your better human. It's something I fight for and work for every day.

I AM A FULL-TIME JOB.
I AM **FAR** FROM DONE.

BETTER HUMAN.

STARTS
TODAY.

RONDA CONGER
AND THE **BETTER HUMAN** ENERGY CREW

#WEDIDIT

PHOTO CREDITS

Unless otherwise stated, all photos and graphics are public domain, Creative Commons licensed or considered fair use.

I especially want to thank Canva.com, iStock.com, Unsplash.com, Freepik.com, Kayla Schill and my friend Google.com for hookin' it up with awesome photography.

All other graphics created by Arielle "hardest-working-shark-loving" Heinonen. My love and thanks. You brought my words to life with your magical skills.

ABOUT THE AUTHOR

Some say she was raised by wolves, others claim truckers. Business woman, professional speaker, and now author of two books: **Better Human** and **Better Thinking** Ronda's high energy and passion are rumored to come from shot-gunning Red Bulls daily, but she'll tell you it comes from her incredibly hot husband (just ask her) and her sons.

She thanks the heavens each day for this incredible journey and is so grateful for the opportunity to serve and love all those that she comes in contact with.

elevate
publishing

A strategic publisher empowering authors to strengthen their brand.

Visit Elevate Publishing for our latest offerings.
www.elevatepub.com